The Perfect Relationship Anxiety Workbook for Married Couples

How Anxiety Destroys Relationships: Stop Feeling Insecure in Love and Worried in a Relationship. Learn to Recognize Anxious Behaviors that Trigger Insecurity.

Kate Homily

A WORD BY THE AUTHOR

I hope you enjoy this book as much as I loved writing it. If you do, it would be wonderful if you could take a short minute and leave a review on Amazon.com and Goodreads.com as soon as you can, as your kind feedback is much appreciated and so very important. Thank you.

Congratulation on downloading this e-book, currently best-selling in Anxiety Disorder & Phobias Category, and thank You for doing so.

Please Enjoy It

© Copyright 2020 - All rights reserved.

The content contained within this book may not be reproduced, duplicated or transmitted without direct written permission from the author or the publisher.

Under no circumstances will any blame or legal responsibility be held against the publisher, or author, for any damages, reparation, or monetary loss due to the information contained within this book, either directly or indirectly.

Legal Notice:

This book is copyright protected. It is only for personal use. You cannot amend, distribute, sell, use, quote or paraphrase any part, or the content within this book, without the consent of the author or publisher.

Disclaimer Notice:

Please note the information contained within this document is for educational and entertainment purposes only. All effort has been executed to present accurate, up to date, reliable, complete information. No warranties of any kind are declared or implied. Readers acknowledge that the author is not engaged in the rendering of legal, financial, medical or professional advice. The content within this book has been derived from various sources. Please consult a licensed professional before attempting any techniques outlined in this book.

By reading this document, the reader agrees that under no circumstances is the author responsible for any losses, direct or indirect, that are incurred as a result of the use of the information contained within this document, including, but not limited to, errors, omissions, or inaccuracies.

Table of Contents

INTRODUCTION **0**

CHAPTER 1: HOW TO USE THIS BOOK **3**

CHAPTER 2: WHAT IS RELATIONSHIP ANXIETY? **8**

   COMMON QUESTIONS REGARDING RELATIONSHIP ANXIETY 10
   DEALING WITH YOUR RELATIONSHIP ANXIETY 13

CHAPTER 3: ARE DOUBTS NORMAL IN A RELATIONSHIP? **18**

   LONG-TERM IMPACTS 22
   WHAT TO REMEMBER 25

CHAPTER 4: WHAT CAUSES ANXIETY AND INSECURITY IN A RELATIONSHIP? **27**

   THE ROOT OF THE PROBLEM 28
      Previous Relationships 29
      Low Self-Esteem 30
      Attachment Style 31
      Loss of Trust 33
      Misunderstanding 34
      Tendency to Question 35

CHAPTER 5: WHAT ARE THE MAIN REASONS FOR CONFLICTS BETWEEN COUPLES? **37**

      Religion 39
      Dominance 39
      Child Bearing 40
      Poor Communication 41
      Materialistic Difficulties 42
      Perception 43
      Values 43

Work-Related Stress *44*
Unwritten Rules *45*
Behavior..*46*

CHAPTER 6: HOW TO UNDERSTAND YOUR PARTNER AND MASTER THE CONFLICTS IN YOUR RELATIONSHIP 47

UNDERSTANDING EACH OTHER 49
RESOLVING ISSUES TOGETHER 52

CHAPTER 7: RECOGNIZING IRRATIONAL BEHAVIORS THAT TRIGGER ANXIETY AND INSECURITY 57

EXAMPLES...60
When Your Partner Doesn't Immediately Reply to Your Text *60*
When Your Partner Can't Spend Time with You...............*61*
When Your Partner Receives a Call or Text *62*
When Your Partner Appears to Be Distant.......................*64*
When Your Partner Takes Jokes Too Far *65*
When Your Partner Won't Propose to You.......................*66*

CHAPTER 8: HOW DO YOU STOP BEING ANXIOUS AND INSECURE IN A RELATIONSHIP? 68

STRATEGIES AND EXERCISES 69

CHAPTER 9: HOW TO USE YOUR RELATIONSHIP ANXIETY TO GROW 79

ESTABLISH A DEEPER CONNECTION 80
SPEND QUALITY TIME TOGETHER..82
GO THE EXTRA MILE 84
LEARN ABOUT THE WARNING SYSTEM 86

CHAPTER 10: IMPROVING SELF-AWARENESS AND SELF-PASSION WITH ANXIETY IN A RELATIONSHIP 89

ACCEPT THAT ANXIETY IS COMMON 92
PRACTICE MINDFULNESS..93
SEEK OUTLETS FOR YOUR THOUGHTS 95
FALL IN LOVE WITH YOURSELF 97
UNDERSTAND EXTERNAL INFLUENCES 99

- Work on Self-Care 101
- Rewire Your Brain 102

CONCLUSION 105

REFERENCES 109

Introduction

"Just when the caterpillar thought the world was ending, she became a butterfly." -Barbara Haines Howett

It is the root of many issues. Anxiety can be difficult to manage on a daily basis. As you try to navigate your feelings, you have likely become entirely overwhelmed, even when things are seemingly okay. This is the way that anxiety can be so powerful, convincing you that you aren't capable of living your life. All of the feelings that anxiety brings forward are heightened when you are in a relationship. Not only are you dealing with your own personal struggles, but you also have to make sure that they do not impact your marriage. In worrying about how you are treating your partner, this can create even more anxiety for you to deal with. The good news is that anxiety can be easily resolved once it is identified.

No matter where your anxiety stems from, you need to realize that you deserve to live in peace. Having a stable and happy marriage is one of the many positive things that you are likely aiming for in your life. This might be easier said than done. If you have been struggling with anxiety for a while, getting into a better mindset is going to be a worthwhile challenge for you. Relationship anxiety can appear during any stage of a relationship, no matter how great things have been going. What you need to avoid is placing the blame on yourself or on your partner. Because this happens naturally, the only thing you should be focusing on is how to fix it.

Many different thoughts have likely passed through your head as you have been dealing with your relationship anxiety. You might be wondering if you are good enough for your partner or if they truly care about you. Deep down, you also might know the answers to these questions, yet your anxiety won't let you believe them. This can become a battle between what you know is right and how your anxiety is trying to mislead you. Your whole focus will eventually turn to you soothing the anxiety instead of devoting your time to your marriage. As you can imagine, this is something that can really wear you down after a while.

Studies have shown that nearly 40 million people suffer from anxiety on a daily basis; 20% of this group feeling anxiety toward their partners. This is a very big statistic, so if you find that you are a part of it, know that you are not alone.

With the help of this guide, you will learn how to confront your anxiety head-on. Instead of feeling that it is controlling you and your marriage, you will understand how to cope with it to preserve your relationship. Knowing that you deserve to live a life that is free of worry, the techniques that you will learn will help you feel that you can handle your anxiety.

My name is Kate Homily, and I am a relationship therapist. With over 18 years of experience, I have seen many cases of relationship anxiety. At one point in my life, I even experienced it for myself. It was a battle for me to overcome, but I made it out on the other side. Through my wisdom, I hope to teach others how they can do the same thing.

Today, I am a happily married mother of three with two rambunctious puppies. It took a lot of hard work to get here, but I now know exactly what it takes to create harmony in my life and marriage. I no longer spend my days worrying about the what-ifs or that my life could fall apart. Instead, I have the time to enjoy all of my blessings and remain thankful for everything that I've accomplished.

going. What you need to avoid is placing the blame on yourself or on your partner. Because this happens naturally, the only thing you should be focusing on is how to fix it.

Many different thoughts have likely passed through your head as you have been dealing with your relationship anxiety. You might be wondering if you are good enough for your partner or if they truly care about you. Deep down, you also might know the answers to these questions, yet your anxiety won't let you believe them. This can become a battle between what you know is right and how your anxiety is trying to mislead you. Your whole focus will eventually turn to you soothing the anxiety instead of devoting your time to your marriage. As you can imagine, this is something that can really wear you down after a while.

Studies have shown that nearly 40 million people suffer from anxiety on a daily basis; 20% of this group feeling anxiety toward their partners. This is a very big statistic, so if you find that you are a part of it, know that you are not alone.

With the help of this guide, you will learn how to confront your anxiety head-on. Instead of feeling that it is controlling you and your marriage, you will understand how to cope with it to preserve your relationship. Knowing that you deserve to live a life that is free of worry, the techniques that you will learn will help you feel that you can handle your anxiety.

My name is Kate Homily, and I am a relationship therapist. With over 18 years of experience, I have seen many cases of relationship anxiety. At one point in my life, I even experienced it for myself. It was a battle for me to overcome, but I made it out on the other side. Through my wisdom, I hope to teach others how they can do the same thing.

Today, I am a happily married mother of three with two rambunctious puppies. It took a lot of hard work to get here, but I now know exactly what it takes to create harmony in my life and marriage. I no longer spend my days worrying about the what-ifs or that my life could fall apart. Instead, I have the time to enjoy all of my blessings and remain thankful for everything that I've accomplished.

Chapter 1:

How to Use this Book

This book will help you by teaching you more about relationship anxiety. Once you are able to better understand it, you will be able to come up with solutions that truly work for your life. This kind of anxiety can be very hard to deal with because it impacts the closest relationship that you have in your life — your relationship with your spouse. You should be able to share your most personal moments with your spouse while being the truest version of yourself. This level of openness is what makes for a fantastic marriage. Even if you are not yet married to your significant other, this book touches on topics that will likely apply to you if you are in a serious relationship.

The topics that are covered in this book are going to apply to women who are struggling with their anxiety levels to the point where it begins to impact their existing relationship. Though the book is geared toward the woman's point of view, it can still be very beneficial for the man to read as well. Relationship anxiety does not discriminate, so you must make sure that you are taking a look at the bigger picture as you evaluate your relationship. Try not to make any judgments as you examine your relationship for these flaws. Know that once you find them, you are going to fix them to make your relationship great and healthy.

You should feel hopeful and ready for the changes that are to come. While any change can be scary, know that a change in your relationship is going to have one goal — to strengthen and improve your bond. As a couple, it can become very easy to mix your lives and your personality traits, forgetting that you are actually both individuals. While marriage is a union, you must remember that you are two separate parts of this union. You have your own feelings, worries, goals, and interests. Do not allow yourself to become so invested in your marriage that you begin to lose sight of who you are as a person. This can be a way that you will trigger your relationship anxiety.

By mastering all of the concepts that you will learn, you should be able to successfully resolve all of your doubts. Any worries that have developed over time will be put to rest. The things that cause you to feel unsure in your relationship will be broken down into ways that allow you to process them for what they truly are. No one else can put you at ease in your relationship except for yourself. Many people make the mistake of relying on their spouse to do this for them, but that is only part of how you will obtain security in your relationship. Your partner should make you feel stable, but you must also feel stable in your own right.

Brushing off these anxiety issues that you are dealing with is never the answer. When you suppress these feelings, they are only going to return in full force at a later date. It isn't fun to live your life this way, never knowing when your anxiety is going to make another appearance. For this reason, utilizing real methods that work to put these feelings to rest will help you overcome them. You aren't going to be pushing them aside for later. The work that you do will actually eliminate the anxiety and provide you with helpful methods for keeping it away. When you know how to soothe yourself, you will be much better at staying calm no matter what happens. Before you even begin working on these issues, you must tell yourself that you want to work on them.

Being open with your partner is a must. If you cannot talk to your partner about the anxiety that you are feeling, then they are going to be confused when you start treating them differently. This can be a big downfall of any marriage because it leaves your partner feeling like they did something wrong. Plenty of times, the anxiety is not even directly related to something that your partner did recently or has done in the past. It stems from an insecurity that you feel inside of yourself. You must understand that you need to get your own negative thoughts under control before you allow them to become a regular part of your relationship dynamic.

The best way to start this conversation is just by being honest. This book aims to help you stay true to yourself. With the techniques that you will learn, you will have a renewed sense of confidence. If you ever have any doubts about how to deal with your anxiety, you can turn to this book for different tips that you can try. The same methods that work for other people won't necessarily work for you and your relationship, but healing from your anxiety does tend to involve a little bit of trial and error. As long as you are willing and committed to the cause, then you should have the confidence to know that you can break through all of your doubts and live your life with the healthiest relationship possible.

Marriage does take a lot of work, but it is all for a worthy cause. Those who are not willing to acknowledge their marital problems end up living with unhappy marriages that will eventually fall apart. If you want to have the strongest marriage possible, you need to be willing to put in this work. Remind yourself why you are working so hard and what your desired end result is going to be. From this point forward, you do not need to be fearful of your anxiety. You can be comfortable and happy knowing that your anxiety will remain under control, leaving only room for you and your partner to grow happily together.

By becoming more educated on the topic, you will be able to feel more hopeful. Being able to read about the actual causes of your anxiety will allow you to see that it is not all in your head; your thoughts and feelings are valid. With a sense of understanding, you and your partner are going to be able to address the roots of these issues. You will no longer be arguing about the same things because you will be able to find solutions to these problems. Without all of the stress that you were once holding onto, you will see how your anxiety will start to fade away. It is a wonderful feeling knowing that you have what it takes to keep yourself and your partner happy.

Chapter 2:

What Is Relationship Anxiety?

At any point during your relationship, you can be subject to anxiety. While it is more common for this anxiety to form in the beginning stages, it does not discriminate. Sometimes, the anxiety can be triggered by certain events or experiences that the two of you have as a couple. No matter where it comes from, you need to be able to pinpoint it so that you can address it. As you know, anxiety that is left untreated can manifest into bigger problems and put a lot of strain onto your relationship. When you are both stressed out, you are more likely to argue and feel that you are not on the same page. This can be very discouraging, especially in marriage. When you want to feel unity, yet you feel like you don't understand one another, this can cause you to second guess your relationship.

It is difficult to narrow down the exact cause for relationship anxiety. Some believe that there is an event that triggers the anxiety, while others believe that it is a combination of factors that lead up to a breaking point. No matter how it forms, being able to recognize that you are acting on your anxious thoughts is important. You might realize that you are secretly questioning your partners intentions even when they have not given you a reason to. You might also start feeling that you are not good enough for your partner, although nothing has actually changed that would lead you to believe this is true. Anxiety can be powerful enough to make you think that there are all of these problems in your relationship when there might not be any problems at all.

For some, relationship anxiety sets in because of the experiences that you've had in the past. If you have ever been in a manipulative or abusive relationship, it is natural to be fearful that your present/future relationships will also be the same. That is a lot of psychological damage for one person to endure, so getting out of that mindset is going to be very difficult. If this situation applies to your life, know that it is not your fault. If anyone has ever treated you less than you deserved, that is merely a reflection of their own character. One of the most common mistakes made is the internalization of the bad things that others have done to us. If you accept these things and hold them inside, your subconscious is always going to return to them.

Remind yourself why you and your spouse got together. Think about how things were the first time you met and when you first started dating. This spark is the reason you decided to get married. While relationships naturally become less exciting as time goes on, those people who fell in love are still the same people. That natural chemistry should still exist, even when the honeymoon stage comes to an end. By reminding yourself of all the qualities that you fell in love with when you met your partner, you should also realize that they feel in love with your qualities too. These little things can often bring you back to that feeling of how it was when you first got together.

Common Questions Regarding Relationship Anxiety

Having doubts is normal with anything that you do in life. Being able to recognize that you might be making the wrong decision can be a very humbling experience. On the other hand, it can show you that you know what is best for you. Having the confidence and the ability to make choices is necessary if you want to really get the most out of your life. The person that you have picked to spend the rest of your life with is a very big decision to make. For this reason, anxiety can start to show up over time as you truly get to know the other person. We all have our flaws, and we are usually only comfortable showing them to our partners after we have been together for some time. At this point in any relationship, it should mean that you both feel comfortable enough to be your true selves. This means that all of your personality traits will be seen, flaws and all.

Your flaws make you human; you can learn from them. We all have things that we need to work on in life, but that doesn't mean that we are unlovable or hard to be with. Your spouse should accept you, even despite these flaws. Their love should remain unconditional. As long as you can work on the things that you have to work on about yourself, then there should be no reason why your spouse wouldn't be willing to accept you for who you are. The following are some typical questions that tend to arise as you begin to develop relationship anxiety. If you have ever thought about these things or even asked your spouse these things, you should be able to identify that you do have anxiety in your relationship.

Are we actually right for one another?

Does my partner love me?

Are we moving too fast?

Are they losing interest in me?

Am I ready for this commitment?

All of these questions are fueled by doubt. While you might have seemingly real reasons to ask these questions, try to think about what is causing the insecurity. When you are in a healthy relationship, you should know exactly how your partner feels about you. Both of you should be on the same page when it comes to the stage of your relationship and how comfortable you are with one another. Any commitments that were made have been made on a mutual level. A marriage can start out this way, yet you might still begin to have certain doubts creep into your mind over time. This is normal, and it is nothing to be ashamed of. If you have ever thought about any of the above questions or anything similar, you are not alone.

These questions tend to come up because you have had a moment of doubt. As you know, doubt can be a common feeling for any big life decision. Taking the time to consider if you are making the right choice shows how important it is to you. What you need to be sure of is that you aren't being fueled by doubt. When you develop relationship anxiety, you have likely been experiencing doubts for a while now. It becomes detrimental to your life and your relationship when you allow yourself to become consumed by it. A relationship that has an underlying tone of doubt is always going to be tense. You might be very defensive over certain things, and your partner might not even know why.

It is important that you get your triggers under control. By learning about the roots of your issues, you should be able to have a better understanding of why you are feeling the way that you do. Think about what caused you to get to this point and try your best to be honest with yourself. When you hold back, you might end up taking your worries out on your partner. This is never a good experience in a relationship because it is only going to create an added source of stress. When you are dealing with relationship anxiety, you will become more focused on these worries than actually being a caring partner. All of your priorities will shift until the anxiety is all that you can think about. Imaginably, this is a very difficult way to live. It will also end up impacting your partner in a negative way.

Dealing with Your Relationship Anxiety

To manage the anxiety that you feel in your relationship, you must take accountability for your actions. When you can recognize that you are acting out of insecurity, take a moment to listen to your inner voice. Do you talk to yourself with respect, or are you being too hard on yourself? The way that you communicate with your subconscious can make a very big impact on the way that you are going to take action. When you are acting out of fear or insecurity, you might make some decisions that you wouldn't normally make if you were thinking clearly. Any time that you begin to feel your anxiety, take a few deep breaths. Breathing is super important when you are dealing with anything stressful. It regulates your body and your mind, allowing you to focus on what is most important.

Once you have changed your mindset, think about the problem again. Does it feel any different now that you've had a moment to separate yourself from it? Worry only tends to build the more that you fuel it. By breathing before reacting, you are giving yourself some space from the problem. Try not to be so critical of yourself. Think about the way that you treat your partner. When they have doubts, you are likely going to be there to provide words of encouragement. Do the same thing for yourself. Know that you deserve the confidence boost just as much as your partner does. Even if you already have a supportive partner, you also need to be able to be there for yourself.

It puts a lot of pressure on your partner when you are constantly unloading problems on them. They are going to be there for you, but you also need to make sure that you are putting in the effort to grow as a person. Recognize that your anxious way of thinking isn't going to be permanent. As long as you are able to keep pushing forward, you should be able to get back into a healthy state of being. This is going to be beneficial both for your relationship and for yourself. Keep in mind that you are always in control of your own happiness. While things might happen to you that try to bring you down, you are ultimately in control of your own feelings.

Make the choice to not let your anxiety win. When you begin to experience relationship anxiety, it can cause you to act differently because of the insecurity that you are feeling. Sometimes, people get clingy and become very needy toward their partners. There are also certain instances when it might make you feel that you need more control in your relationship. If you were to act on either of these things, you can imagine the impact that it would make on your partner. Being a control freak or a clingy partner is not going to make your anxiety go away. You might feel better temporarily, but it is still going to be there below the surface.

When you can see that you are gravitating toward negative self-talk, stop yourself. Do not let these thoughts even enter your brain or else they will only grow stronger. Know that you have the choice to either allow this negative self-talk to occur or to redirect it. When you redirect it, you can take the original thought you had and put a more positive spin on it. For example, if you feel like your partner doesn't love you anymore, think about all of the reasons why your partner has said that they have fallen in love with you. Even if time has passed, or if you have been married for a while, remember these small joys because they are still relevant.

If you tend to think that your partner is stuck with you and that they could find someone better, remind yourself that your partner has free will. Your partner can do anything at any time, but they have chosen to commit to you. Take this commitment as a sign of them wanting to be with you, so there is no need to question it. When you worry about problems that don't truly exist, you are giving your anxiety plenty of room to grow. When you take away these negative thoughts and replace them with positive facts, you are taking the power away from your anxiety. This is exactly what you need to do to remind yourself that you are in control of your happiness. You can decide how you are going to talk to yourself and how you are going to treat your partner.

Try to let go of any negativity that you are currently holding onto. You can do so by practicing some breathing techniques and giving yourself the space to clear your head. Spending time alone is healthy, even when you are married. You are an individual with your own set of needs, so make sure that you aren't ignoring them. Only 10 minutes of breathing or meditation can make a huge difference in the way that you feel. Try to focus on the things that you love about yourself and the things that your partner says they love about you. Push aside any of the worries that keep trying to pop up. Remind yourself that your partner has chosen you for a reason, just as you have chosen them.

When you choose to work on yourself from the inside out, this is going to create the biggest change in your mindset. Being able to feel great about yourself and have that renewed sense of confidence is going to make you a better partner. You have likely heard the saying before, but it remains true — if you can't love yourself, then you won't be able to love someone else. Self-love often gets pushed to the back burner when you enter a serious relationship. Make sure that you remind yourself of how important it is. Take some time regularly to unwind by yourself so that you don't lose sight of who you are as an individual.

Chapter 3:

Are Doubts Normal in a Relationship?

We have talked a little bit about doubts and why you feel them, but you might be wondering if they are normal to feel if you are in a committed relationship. What is most important to remember when it comes to feeling doubtful is that you don't need to panic. If a doubt arises while you are in a relationship, this is just your brain picking up on signals that either make you worried or displeased. It is normal to feel doubtful sometimes, even if you are in a wonderful relationship. You are a human being, so you are going to likely feel this way at some point in time. What matters most is where this doubt is actually stemming from and how you decide to handle it.

Many psychologists agree that even the healthiest couples can feel normal instances of doubt and anxiety at times. Much like anxiety, doubt can also happen at any point during the relationship. A lot of people experience doubts in the beginning, but it is also possible to experience them when you are already married and have been for a long time. Anything that leads you to second-guess yourself is a trigger that should be examined. For example, if you begin to doubt that your partner's feelings for you are as strong as they once were, ask yourself what has led you to this conclusion. Once you get to the bottom of the problem, you should be able to take a closer look at why this thought has surfaced in your mind.

Insecurity often fuels doubt. If you believe that your partner doesn't have strong feelings for you anymore, you are likely going to equate this to them being interested in someone else or you not being enough for them. Unless they have actually said these things to you, then you should not allow your mind to run with these ideas. Only allow yourself to think about the concrete facts. Has your partner cheated? Have they told you that you are not good enough for them? If you cannot answer yes to these questions, then you should not have to spend any more time dwelling on these things. Convince yourself to let go of them.

There are certain cases when anxiety can be helpful in a relationship. If you have ever felt butterflies in the early stages of your relationship, this is actually a form of anxiety. Most people feel it as excitement rather than negativity, though. When you and your partner were first getting to know one another, things likely felt very exciting and new. You were discovering all of each other's qualities and learning how to come together as a couple. Each time that you learned something new about your partner or experienced something that brought you closer together, you likely felt these butterflies and took them as a positive sign.

Because you already know one another very well, any feelings of anxiety that develop after you have already been in the relationship for a while are going to feel more bothersome. This is the perfect time for doubts to creep in, preying on your overthinking mind. Pair this with the negative self-talk, and you have a very high chance of making yourself miserable in your relationship. Being with a partner who is struggling can be very difficult, and sometimes, unfair. Keeping yourself in touch with reality is going to prevent you from allowing your doubts to take over. Any negative voices that you hear in your head can be silenced with some positive self-talk.

The more that you choose to focus on your anxiety, the less you are focusing on your actual relationship. As you know, relationships take a lot of effort. When you don't pay attention to your partner and instead pay attention to these problems that you believe need to take priority, you might actually end up transforming into the kind of partner that you are fearful of. Nobody wants to be with someone who isn't considerate of their feelings or attentive to their needs. It becomes difficult to fill these roles for your partner when all you can do is worry about the what-ifs. If something isn't actually happening in your relationship right at the moment, then you shouldn't panic over it.

When you overanalyze things, you are actually distancing yourself from your partner because you are viewing your relationship as a big speculative situation. Instead of seeing your relationship and your partner for what they truly are, you will be acting on fears and worries that might not even actually exist. This is a very exhausting way to live, and it can be damaging to your mental health. Not to mention, it will drive distance between yourself and your partner. None of these things are worth it, so the choice should be very clear when you realize that you can reframe the way that you think. Instead of bringing your worst fears to life, focus on the good things that you already have. Try to attract more of these good things into your life and your relationship.

Long-Term Impacts

You are now realizing how damaging doubtful behavior and relationship anxiety truly can become. If you have been experiencing either for a long time, or if you allow it to get out of control, you are going to be subject to many different problems that are proven to be difficult to overcome. Starting with emotional distress, this will become your permanent state of mind. If you have ever been in emotional distress before, you will know how damaging it can be when it is not treated for a long time. Being in any kind of distress is not healthy for you, and it will not make you a good partner. You will be so caught up in your negative feelings that you likely will not have the time to think about what you can be doing for your partner.

Emotional distress can also lead to some serious mental health issues, such as depression or even thoughts of suicide. When you are constantly viewing your situation with such a negative outlook, you might lose sight of what you are grateful for in your life. Things can seem confusing and scary with no real purpose. This kind of thinking becomes very dangerous because you can easily lead yourself to believe that there is no happy outcome for you or your relationship. Even when nothing at all has happened, your mind is still powerful enough to convince you that your relationship is a disaster. This is why learning how to control your mindset is crucial.

You might begin to lose your motivation in your relationship. This can manifest in many different ways. An upsetting feeling is when you lose all sexual or romantic motivation, leading your partner to believe that they have done something wrong. In reality, you might just be too caught up in your own doubts or anxiety to be able to be there for your partner in this way. Naturally, this can cause a big divide between two people who are in a committed relationship. You might also lose your motivation in other ways, such as being there for your partner. Without your support, your partner might also be led to believe that they have done something wrong or that they have upset you in some way.

When you don't have the motivation, your relationship is going to feel very stagnant. If you are already out of the honeymoon stage, this can really make or break your relationship. With no direction, you aren't going to be focused on moving forward with your partner. Instead, you are likely only going to get stuck in the same habits and routines. This can become very cumbersome, especially if your partner has goals in mind for the future. When only one person is putting in effort toward goals that concern both of you, this can be a very discouraging situation to face. Make sure that you are letting your partner know exactly where you stand on your future and your goals together.

Don't forget how taxing emotional pain can become. When you are constantly fighting with your own emotions, you are bound to become physically exhausted in the process. Fatigue is a very common sign that you are stressing yourself out on a regular basis. Depression can also lead you to this feeling. You might not even feel like you have enough energy to get out of bed each day when you begin to feel the weight from your fatigue. This can be very upsetting for your partner because they will feel helpless. It will also likely upset you more because you won't have the energy to interact with them or reassure them like you once did.

Exhaustion isn't the only physical symptom for you to look out for. If you begin to experience stomach problems, your stress likely has something to do with them. When you are unhappy, your digestive system tends to become very reactive. Even small meals can upset your stomach, causing you to become averse to certain foods. This can lead to some very unhealthy eating habits if you aren't careful. Once your body starts to go downhill, you can bet that your mind will be following closely. Without a healthy body, not only are you going to be unable to be there for your partner like you once were, but your work and other responsibilities are also going to suffer.

When your stomach isn't feeling well, other people are likely going to take notice. This can become an added source of stress because you likely don't want others to know that you are having any problems at all. One of the worst parts about experiencing relationship doubts or anxiety is the shame in knowing that it is happening. Many people will go to great lengths to hide this from others in an attempt to make it seem like they are in a perfect relationship. Know that perfection doesn't exist. You can be in a great relationship, but you and your partner aren't always going to see eye to eye; that's normal. Be realistic with yourself and others because there is no shame in that. You are only human.

What to Remember

Overall, it wouldn't be realistic to say that you will never feel doubts about your relationship. Make sure that you open your mind to the idea that some doubts can be normal, as long as you do not always take them seriously. Before you decide to react to these doubts that pop into your mind, first see if you can locate the source of them. If you cannot, then it is not worth getting upset over. You might end up realizing what the source is and finding an immediate solution. This would mean that your panic and worry happened for no good reason.

Prove to yourself that you can self-soothe when you are in situations where the doubts want to take over. Remind yourself of the concrete facts about your relationship and what it is that you are worried about. If you can't prove it, then it is not a fact. Any remaining insecurities are to be examined. Think about the issues that you are left with. Ask yourself if these are things that you need to deal with or if they are things that you need to discuss with your partner. From there, the choice should be easy to make. When you simplify the process for yourself, all of your doubts won't seem as overwhelming as they once did.

Know that you have everything that you need to get through these moments of doubt. Also, remind yourself that it is natural to feel this way, as everyone is going to experience some moments of weakness. Whether something happened that triggered your doubts or you simply talked yourself into a corner, know that you can just as easily guide yourself to a more positive mindset. When you have positivity, you have a fighting chance of managing your problems. You will also be more likely to find a healthy way to approach this. "Fixing" self-destructive behavior with more self-destructive behavior isn't a solution at all.

Be aware not only of how you are treating your partner but of how you are treating yourself. Both of these are very important components of being a great partner. If you cannot treat yourself with respect, then that is sending your partner mixed messages about the way that you are going to treat them. Any worries that arise should be addressed and handled accordingly. You don't need to dwell on things to fix them. By having a clear understanding of your issues from the very beginning, you should be able to come to a quick solution. The more that you practice this, the better you will get at it. You will find that both you and your partner will be able to grow together when you aren't being chained down by doubts.

Chapter 4:

What Causes Anxiety and Insecurity in a Relationship?

In this chapter, you are going to get a more detailed look at what exactly causes your anxiety and insecurity. While it can stem from many different things, even a combination of several things, you need to understand how it happens for yourself personally. You are going to learn about the basics and have a better understanding of where these feelings start. By having this knowledge and this perspective, you should be able to swiftly avoid these things to avoid becoming anxious again in the future. Taking a look at the given examples, you will likely find that you can identify with a lot of them, if not most of them. Don't think about this as a negative thing. Instead, you can think about all of the progress that you are about to make.

The Root of the Problem

Before you work on fixing the problem, you must be able to identify it. While it is often a bad choice to be critical of yourself, in this case, it becomes necessary. To deal with the issues that you are having in your relationship, you must be able to identify exactly what is causing them. Turn inward to see if you can get to the root of your problem. Ask yourself why you are choosing to behave the way that you are. There are no right or wrong answers for this step. No matter how you are feeling, even if it is extreme, you must have a reason for it. Know that this might not be the healthiest choice, but it will soon become a curbed behavior.

If you try to apply all of the different fixes that you know, this is only going to be a waste of time and energy. Don't become frustrated because you aren't seeing an improvement in yourself or your relationship.

Take a more targeted approach. See if you can get down to the very bottom of your problems, identifying them and seeing them for what they really are. It can be scary to face your problems in this way, but this is the way that you are going to be able to fix them. Know that you need to trust in yourself and that you need to trust in the process. Problem-solving is difficult for a reason, but you will be happy with the end result. When you only solve the surface layer of problems, the rest of them are bound to come up later. It makes sense to get down to the root of things.

Previous Relationships

If you have ever been in a relationship in which you were mistreated, you are naturally going to be cautious of this in the future. It is a defensive mechanism that is normal for any abused individual to take on. However, it becomes a problem when you start to place this role on your partner, even when they are not abusive. Your constant fear and judgment will eventually lead your partner to many negative feelings, from insecurity to anger. It doesn't feel great to be accused of being controlling or manipulative when you aren't.

Make sure that any fears you have surrounding this issue are grounded in reality. If you have ever been broken up with unexpected, cheated on, physically or mentally abused, or lied to, then you are more likely to develop this kind of anxiety. When you are wronged so badly, it often has the ability to shake you to your core and change you as a person. What you must learn is that you need to heal from the past instead of comparing your present relationship to something that could end up the same way.

To convince yourself that you are being mistreated again, you will often go out of your way to look for "signs" that your partner is not good for you. Whenever you have to search for these things, they are likely not based in reality. You will know if your partner is doing something wrong from the actions that they present to you. Understandably, if you have been manipulated in the past, this can give you trust issues. Again, you need to keep these fears under control instead of taking them out on your partner. If you doubt your partner so strongly, this could be a sign that the relationship is not healthy for you. If your partner is late to get home from work, and the first thing you think is that they were cheating on you, then you should be able to see this as a sign of your anxiety taking over your way of thinking.

Low Self-Esteem

When you have low self-esteem, this can present itself in many ways. Having low-self esteem often comes with many insecurities. Whether you are insecure about the way you look or your ability to please your partner, you will find that you will start projecting your issues. For example, if you feel disappointed in yourself, you will also start projecting this feeling and will start to believe that your partner is also disappointed in you. The way to tell if you are projecting or not is if your partner has expressed this to you themselves. If they have not indicated their disappointment, then this feeling is coming from your own anxiety and being projected.

As you can imagine, it becomes very unfair when you start to accuse your partner of feeling certain ways when they insist that they do not. It can become a very exhausting battle to fight, one that often proves that it isn't worth it. You will know when you are projecting feelings onto your partner when they constantly feel that they have to prove to you how much they love you or how they see you. Reassurance is important in a relationship, but if they are constantly spending their time reassuring you, this can become exhausting. No matter what answer you receive from them, it likely won't be enough to fix your low self-esteem.

You need to work on bettering yourself, not only your relationship. Realize that you are an individual person with individual needs. You need to be able to look at yourself in the mirror and be happy with what you see and the person that you are. When you feel anything less than this, there will be a risk of you projecting the negative feelings onto your partner. Make sure that you prioritize self-care. Understand that it is not selfish or excessive; it is necessary for your own mental health.

Attachment Style

An attachment style is something that develops when you are a child. Depending on how you are raised, you can either have a healthy sense of how to bond with someone or you might feel that you constantly need to receive reassurance to know that you are cared for. This is definitely something that can end up being projected as you reach adulthood and get into serious relationships. Even though these decisions were made by your parents, they will impact you for the rest of your life.

If your parents were cold and withheld affection, you might have developed a habit of hiding your emotions and needs. Babies who are left to cry for extended periods of time learn how to self-soothe. This can be a difficult process, as they are taught that no one is going to come for them when they are in need. As translated into adulthood, you might feel this way about your partner or you might even believe that your feelings are not important.

Having an anxious attachment means that you are living in fear that your partner could leave you at any moment. These abandonment issues usually stem from having a parent do the same thing during childhood. Children who come from broken homes can often grow to believe that every person in their life is not permanent. If you feel this way, you are never going to feel secure with your spouse because you will be constantly waiting for them to abandon you.

Alternatively, there is an avoidant attachment style. This occurs when you are the one who keeps your partner at a distance, not revealing too many feelings or providing reassurance. This attachment style can make you appear to be cold or not as invested in the relationship, even when you want to be. No matter what kind of attachment style you have, if it is unhealthy and impacting your relationship, therapy will become very beneficial to you. Being able to sort through your issues and understand why you feel this way will provide you with clarity.

Loss of Trust

You can lose trust in your partner for a variety of reasons. It is the way that you handle this feeling that will ultimately determine if it is a problem or not. Typically, when someone loses their trust in another person, that person will have to prove themselves trustworthy again. If you feel that you are too disappointed by their actions to forgive them, or if you choose to live your life while constantly punishing them for what they did, this is an indication that you are being led by your anxiety.

If you constantly feel a sense of disappointment or negativity, it might be possible that you entered the relationship with this mindset. Not having any faith in your partner can be devastating as the years go on. Both of you will feel that your efforts do not matter. By constantly expecting the end of your relationship, you are going to develop a very apathetic mindset. This can form as a defense mechanism, but it is not the healthiest way to deal with your trust issues.

When you can work together with your partner on these trust issues, your relationship is going to stand a fighting chance. Are there concrete reasons why you no longer trust your partner? If you cannot think about factual reasons why your partner is untrustworthy, you might have to turn your focus inward. What is making *you* feel this way and why? Before you react to the surface issues, it is important to get down to the deeper meaning behind the problem. Allow yourself to explore these feelings and realize that they might be stemming from a warped perception of the relationship that you have created. Even if you want the relationship to last, it is going to be difficult when you cannot set aside your negativity. These anxious thoughts are going to eat away at you constantly, providing a distraction. This won't be fair to either of you.

Misunderstanding

Fighting is a normal part of any healthy relationship. Couples should not get along 24/7, even if they are very similar or have a strong bond. By disagreeing, you are showing that you are still individuals. Being able to stand up for what you believe in is important, even if you are standing up to your spouse. When two adults that love each other get into a disagreement, they should also be able to communicate through the issue. This does not signify that the relationship is doomed, but that can often be what your anxiety leads you to believe.

There are certain types of fighting that can be dangerous. This usually happens when anger becomes physical. If you cannot talk about your feelings without getting overly angry, this is going to lead to something bad. Another bad sign is getting into additional disagreements while you are trying to solve the original one. This could indicate that a misunderstanding is taking place. Getting the right words out can be difficult, but you should be able to do so when you are talking to your partner. If they misunderstand you, correct them. Letting things make you even angrier is not going to solve your problem.

All healthy couples must be able to talk their way through fights, even if misunderstandings occur. Both people should be able to express themselves individually without being talked over. If you realize that your discussions usually do not follow this guideline, then you likely need to work on your conflict resolution skills. Be accountable for your own actions and realize when you are being out of line. You aren't always going to be right, no matter how much you believe that you are. Being able to realize that you are wrong can be a big saving grace when you are working through a misunderstanding with your partner.

Tendency to Question

Do you ever overthink situations? When you are given a decision, does it take you a long time to make up your mind? As a partner, being this way likely means that you are also going to question your significant other a lot to best make your decisions. Asking questions isn't always a negative thing; receiving these answers will provide you with clarity. This becomes detrimental to your relationship when you are unable to trust or believe in your partner. Your questions will begin to sound accusatory, which can lead to defensive responses on their end. Telling the truth and not being believed is an incredibly frustrating problem to face, especially coming from the person who is supposed to love and accept you for who you are.

If you are an over-thinker, you will have the ability to quickly create different scenarios in your head of what *could* be possible. For example, focusing on every detail of your spouse's behavior might lead you to an incorrect conclusion that they are being dishonest with you. When you get into this mindset and begin to convince yourself of things that are not backed by valid facts, this is when your behavior is going to be classified as unhealthy. Realize that placing these labels on your partner is unfair.

To correct this problem, you need to shift your focus. Realize that your partner is an individual with a different way of thinking. What they say to you, and the actions that they choose to display, should be the two forms of communication that you should be holding onto. Try to let go of the what-ifs or the various scenarios that you create in your head. If your partner appears to be genuine with you, then you should not have to go on a quest to find a reason why they might not be. Just because you are prone to looking at negative outcomes does not mean that your partner is automatically going to fulfill them. You need to have trust and faith in them.

Chapter 5:

What Are the Main Reasons for Conflicts between Couples?

When you are in a serious relationship with another person, you are going to have different opinions frequently. The way that you handle these opinions will showcase the health of your relationships. Not all conflicts are bad, and not all conflicts stem from anxiety. There are plenty of cases when conflict can be healthy. It can show you both differing opinions on the same topic, causing you to re-think your stance on the issue. Even if you do not change your opinion, you should be willing to listen to one another in a respectful way. Those who do not listen to one another tend to engage in conflicts more frequently. These are the kind that can become a burden to any relationship.

This chapter is going to take a look at some of the most common reasons for experiencing conflict in a serious relationship. If you can relate to any of these reasons, then you can consider this the first step toward identifying your problems. As a couple, you should be able to communicate through any problem that you encounter. You do not need to engage in a fight or an argument just because you have differing opinions on a topic. Try your best to remain open-minded, treating your partner the way you wish to be treated. Allow them to express themselves without interrupting them or interjecting with your own opinion. Once you have both had the chance to speak, you should then be able to analyze each side and come to an agreement.

Conflict resolution isn't always going to be direct or simple, but as a healthy couple, you should be able to move past your differences to come to an agreement. When you both want a positive outcome, you are both going to be working toward finding a solution. Those that just want to hash it out are often left disappointed or with unresolved feelings. Both of these feelings can prove to be negative when you suppress them, only to return to them during a later conflict that you encounter. These issues can build up in a very unhealthy way if they are not dealt with properly.

Religion

A topic that often comes with strong opinions, couples can definitely start conflicts over religious beliefs. Whether one of you is religious and the other is not, or you and your partner practice religions, there is a chance that this issue can get brought up during an argument. A lot of the time, issues with religion can be tied to how you plan on raising your children or how your family plays a role in your life.

Understandably, having disagreements about religion can lead to some very tense situations. No matter what you or your spouse believes in, both of you must have respect for one another's beliefs. Any healthy relationship comes with a sense of understanding for each other. If you are intolerant of your partner, then you are contributing to the problem of having conflicts. You need to be able to look at your partner's views as valid, just as you see your own views. Taking an intolerant stance becomes very unhealthy for a long-term relationship, often causing unfixable damage.

Dominance

There are typically roles that are taken in any relationship. Usually, one partner takes a more dominant approach, while the other takes on a submissive role. It would be unfair to assume that either one of you *has* to take on these roles, though. The healthiest relationships have a shared sense of dominance. When only one person is dominant, this places the other person at risk of being controlled while in the relationship. Dominance can appear in the form of who takes care of the household and who makes the decisions. It makes sense that a couple should share these duties, even when one of them typically takes on the role themselves.

There is nothing wrong with settling into these roles, but having the flexibility to do things differently is a sign of a healthy relationship. You will realize that there are dominance issues when one of you protests a change in roles. If this makes you feel lesser than or insignificant, then you are likely in need of some work toward your self-esteem. Understand that dominance does not have to be set in stone. Use your own strengths to your advantage by stepping up when you know that it would be beneficial.

Child Bearing

Planning a family is a huge decision to be made by a couple. It comes along with a lot of pressure and being on the same page is essential. Each of you might have your own opinions and preferences when it comes to how many children you would like to have and how you plan on raising them. If you cannot come to an agreement on these decisions, conflict is definitely going to arise. You need to make sure that you are able to compromise when you disagree.

The birth of a child can also come along with many stressors that will test your limits as a couple. When you are both feeling fatigued and overworked, this opens the door for arguments to occur. If you are not careful, you will become very critical of one another. There is also the possibility of becoming stressed out by your lack of finances. Raising a child isn't cheap and if you have not planned adequately, you will struggle. It is very important that you talk to your partner in a realistic way about how you plan on bringing a child into the world.

Poor Communication

Being able to talk to your spouse is important, but making sure that you respect and understand one another is critical. So often, couples feel that they have great communication skills, yet they are still driven apart by disagreements. Remember, talking is only one-half of your communication skills. The other half comes from your listening abilities. Be an active listener at all times. If you are distracted or unwilling to listen, you are not going to see the bigger picture.

If you ever get into a disagreement, you can test your communication skills by how quickly you are able to end it. Those who have poor communication will raise their voices, insult one another, and even bring up past issues that should have already been resolved. This is why you should always aim to work on your problems immediately. If you wait, you will begin to suppress them. While you won't always agree on everything, you do need to know that there are boundaries that should not be crossed. Having respect for one another will keep you both in line.

Materialistic Difficulties

Even if you do not consider yourself a materialistic individual, your material possessions can drive you apart from your spouse. After you get married, most of your material items are shared. There can be a sense of competitiveness that arises when you realize that one of you is contributing more than the other. Alternatively, you might be tempted to compare what you have to what other couples have. Know that your lifestyle and relationship is unique; your success is not dependent on these material possessions.

If you find that your arguments are stemming from what you both have as a couple, you will realize that too much focus is being placed on material items. You can try to get back to what you love about being together, minus these possessions. Think about why you fell in love with your spouse in the first place. If you didn't have anything except for each other, you would appreciate one another for the qualities that you each possess instead of the items that you can procure. Conflicts can become very messy when you realize that you are simply fighting over things that are temporary.

Perception

You and your partner might see the exact same situation differently, and that is normal. While you are a couple, you also need to remember that you are two separate individuals. Your opinions are going to differ. What you need to do is make sure that you understand where your spouse stands on the topics that matter to you. Part of love is being able to accept one another for who you are, not attempting to change your partner so that their views align exactly with your own. There is a fine line between compatibility and control.

As a general rule of thumb, you should openly discuss the things that you value most. If you find that you and your partner see things differently, try to understand their perspective instead of trying to change their mind. This is going to open dialog rather than a disagreement. You might even find that you will be able to understand them better. This kind of mutual respect is very healthy for a relationship, and it shows that you can still love one another, even if you see certain things differently.

Values

As mentioned above, the things that are most important to you are the things that you value most. There are no right or wrong answers when it comes to these topics. Just as you have your own reasons for why you value what you do, so does your spouse. When these values are not aligned or understood, this opens the door for conflict. This kind of conflict can create difficulties because you will both potentially become stubborn as you try to fight for your cause.

Much like your perception, you need to be able to hear one another out on why you value the things that you do. Try to come from a place of understanding rather than a place of judgment. If you find that your core values do not match, you need to evaluate your relationship to see if you can come to a middle ground. Intolerance is only going to promote unhealthy behaviors and lead to more fighting. Talk about big topics, such as your lifestyle, responsibilities, and religions.

Work-Related Stress

No matter what you do for a living, there will be times when your job is going to stress you out. Being able to keep your work life and your personal life balanced is very important. Your partner should be someone that you can vent to about work without taking your frustrations out on them. Your behavior can become unhealthy very quickly if you realize that you are in a bad mood and are treating your spouse differently because of something that happened at work. It is unfair to subject your partner to this kind of treatment.

Know that when you leave work, you need to try to keep the problems that you cannot control at work. If you bring these worries and stressors home with you, they are bound to appear in your personal life.

Overworking is another thing that tends to drive couples apart. If you are too career-oriented, you are going to be lacking in your marriage. Your partner should be someone who will support you and your goals, yet you need to realize that the stress that you encounter during this time is to no fault of your spouse.

Unwritten Rules

Every couple has a set of "rules" in place whether they realize it or not. For example, you should know that if you behave a certain way, this is going to upset your spouse. When you cross these boundaries, not only are you going to upset your partner, but you are going to create a rift in your trust. Betrayal is one of the worst feelings to face, especially from the person who is never supposed to betray you. It can be difficult to create these boundaries when they aren't frequently discussed.

To ensure that you are being fair to your partner, you need to vocalize the things that you are not okay with. This takes away the guesswork and defines a clear line between what you find acceptable and unacceptable. Encourage your partner to do the same thing with you. You might feel that these are things your spouse should already know automatically, but if their actions suggest they do not, you need to tell them. It is healthy for couples to redefine their boundaries, no matter how long they've been married.

Behavior

The way that you behave sends your spouse a very clear message. Even if you are not doing anything that you feel directly impacts your marriage, your actions will speak louder than words. If you cannot do something in front of your spouse, then you should not be doing it when your spouse isn't present. Much like violating the unwritten rules that you have in place, violating certain behavioral patterns can feel just like a betrayal. This will definitely lead to more conflicts and disagreements.

Know that you shouldn't feel controlled by your spouse or vice versa. As long as you both have mutual respect for one another, you should each understand how to act in a way that honors your marriage. This is a tricky balance to find, even for those who have been together for a while. Keep in mind that feelings can also change over the years. The best thing to do is to speak up if your spouse does something that upsets you. This will make it clear as to what you did not care for. Together, you can work on these things.

Chapter 6:

How to Understand Your Partner and Master the Conflicts in Your Relationship

After reading about all of the things that could cause conflict, the thought of working through things with your spouse might feel overwhelming. Know that it does not have to be. By having an accurate understanding of how your partner feels and what they value in life, you will be able to make the best decisions for your marriage together. While you have your own values and morals, you have also agreed to engage in a partnership. This means that you must still work together on the issues that you disagree on. If you only pay attention to the ways that you are compatible, the differences are going to divide you over time. It is just as important to discuss the things that you have differing opinions on as it is to celebrate your similarities.

Couples who are able to keep this duality in their marriage are couples who last. You will each feel a lot happier when you are respected and understood. This chapter is going to help you both in different ways. If you have relationship anxiety, it is going to provide you with concrete ways to ease your worries and to identify the things that are causing you to worry in the first place. For your partner, it will allow them to better understand where you are coming from and how to create more reassurance in the relationship. When paired together, you will be dealing with your conflicts in a much healthier and smarter way.

Understanding Each Other

While you might have relationship anxiety, you need to remember that your partner might not. Because of this, your partner might not be able to relate to the things that you are worried about. This is not because they do not care about you or your feelings but simply because they do not understand how you are feeling. Alternatively, your partner might be able to relate, but they communicate their anxiety in different ways than you do. No matter what the case is, try your best to be understanding of where they are coming from. It might seem incredibly difficult, but the easiest way to rid yourself of your anxiety is to talk about it. Allow your partner to have some insight as to how you are feeling, even if you don't know exactly why.

If you choose to keep your anxiety inside, it is only going to build over time. When you are least expecting it, all of your feelings can be triggered by a minor conflict or disagreement, which will cause even more conflict. You should not feel that you have to deal with your relationship anxiety alone, especially when it pertains to your marriage. Know that you are only half of your marriage; your partner plays just as big of a role as you do. For the sake of being fair to both yourself and your spouse, you need to work hard at describing what you are feeling as soon as you feel it. Get to the root of the problem before it starts to spiral.

When your partner is the one experiencing relationship anxiety, know that this is a very real disorder. It is not something that they are consciously choosing to do, even though it might seem easier to just not think about these things. Your partner is worrying because the relationship matters to them. Try not to put them down or insinuate that their feelings are invalid. Do your best to listen to them and to try to put yourself in their shoes. Be a reassuring and supportive partner to help them work through their anxiety. Even if the worries seem ridiculous, hear them out. When you are able to see things from your partner's perspective, this is going to give you a better understanding of their mindset.

Talking about issues that create anxiety can be very difficult, no matter if you are the one experiencing them or not. You need to know how to talk to one another in a way that isn't aggressive or aggravated. Show each other compassion and treat yourself the way that you would like to be treated. It is likely that the anxious individual is going to be speaking emotionally, while the non-anxious individual will try to speak from a logical standpoint. These are two very different approaches, but you will be able to learn a lot about one another once you can identify who is ruled by emotions and who is ruled by logic. You should aim to live your life by both — inquire about your emotions, yet incorporate logic into your decision-making.

The non-anxious partner might need to take a step back when discussing certain issues. To them, nothing is going to seem like it is as big of a deal. The anxious partner will likely already know that their worries stem from situations that are exaggerated in their own head, but that does not mean that they should be made to feel bad about thinking this way; they can't help it. Do your best to really listen to one another and hear both perspectives before you try to fix the problem. When you talk this way, both of you will feel like you are being heard and respected.

Remember that, most of the time, this anxiety does not stem from anything that is personal. Neither one of you needs to be labeled as a bad guy if one of you is experiencing relationship anxiety. Also, neither one of you needs to take a defensive approach. Being accusatory or acting on fear is likely going to end up with one of you saying or believing something that is irrational. The idea that your spouse could leave you due to your behavior, or vice versa, should never be used as a threat. This is a big sign that the relationship is unhealthy. You should be able to talk openly about your feelings without worrying that you are going to say or do something that will cause your partner to leave.

When you are able to truly understand one another, you will feel that your harmony has been restored. Instead of living with your worries and fears, you will be able to put them to rest and focus on the things that you have going for you. A relationship should be a happy part of your life, not one that causes you grief. If you are truly struggling with your feelings, don't keep them inside. Take a deep breath and have an honest conversation with your spouse. When you do, you are already taking a big step toward relieving yourself of your relationship anxiety.

Also, understand that this is going to be one big process. You won't be able to solve all of your problems after having only one conversation. Get into the habit of checking in with one another. Realistically, you will know that talking about an issue only once might not be enough to fully resolve it. After each talk that you have, give yourself some time to think about the things that you discussed. You might also find that your feelings change or your viewpoints are broadened. This is why having follow-up conversations is also essential. Working on your problems together will allow you to feel that you are both contributing equally to the marriage.

Resolving Issues Together

The next step in your process will be learning how to resolve issues together. If you feel any kind of tension or difference in opinions, have a candid talk with your spouse. You do not need to wait until a problem develops before you talk about something that is bothering you. This will prevent you from worrying about issues that you might be intensifying in your head. Either one of you should be able to start the conversation at any time. When you get into this habit, you will be able to manage the anxiety that you once felt. Know that your conversations should be safe spaces where you are able to fully express yourselves.

As a couple, you can both do your best to research the topic of relationship anxiety so that you can each have a better understanding of it. This will make it less scary and less stressful. When you both feel that you are working together at solving the problem, you will be able to feel a true sense of partnership. This is also going to help you avoid experiencing relationship anxiety in the future. Healthy habits are going to continue to yield healthy results. You can be proud of yourselves for knowing that you are working together on this issue rather than struggling with it independently.

The following are some examples of certain conflicts and how to avoid making mistakes while dealing with them:

1. **Being Brutally Honest:** Being too harsh with one another isn't going to solve your conflicts. In fact, it is almost always going to create additional conflicts for you to deal with. Remember to focus on compassion rather than convincing. If you truly respect one another, you should be able to respect where you are each coming from. When a person with relationship anxiety is met with brutal honesty, this can cause them to shut down or to become flustered. Try to keep the mood as lighthearted as possible, even when you are talking about important issues. As long as you are both reaching for the same result, you will be able to

come together. You can be direct without being offensive or defensive.

2. **Only Sharing Feelings:** You might be wondering if sharing feelings is what you are *supposed* to be doing and it is, in a sense. But don't forget that you need to also share with your partner why you are feeling the way that you do. If you are constantly complaining or expressing your emotions without giving your partner some insight into what is causing you to feel this way, this can create problems in your marriage. They won't know how they are supposed to help you or what they need to do to make things better. Be as specific as possible! Practice your best communication skills.

3. **Getting Defensive:** When your partner expresses an opinion that directly contradicts your own, it can be hard to remain neutral as they start to explain why they feel the way that they do. You have likely had moments where you interrupted your partner or cut them off to explain why your opinion is the right opinion. This is a nearly guaranteed way to start an argument. Respect your partner and their opinions, even when they are different from your own. This kind of tolerance shows them that you value how they feel and that you care about what they have to say. Once you hear

both sides of the issue, you can then discuss it. By doing so, you will both find it easier to come to a middle ground.

4. **Not Asking Questions:** Being an agreeable partner is a redeeming quality, but it can backfire if you are too passive. A lot of mistakes that couples make is that they never question one another. While this might keep the relationship free of conflict at the moment, it is only going to create issues that will come up later on. If your partner says something that you do not understand, for whatever reason, ask them about it. Ask them to explain where they are coming from or why they feel the way that they do. When you have a genuine desire to achieve clarity, you are actually going to be able to resolve your conflict. Asking questions to be condescending is only going to add more fuel to the fire.

5. **Being Too Definitive:** When you use language that includes always/never, you are sending your partner a message that states you do not believe there is a solution to the problem that you are facing. If your partner does something that upsets you, it is best to avoid saying "you ALWAYS" do this or you "are constantly" doing that. Try to pinpoint exactly when your partner has been doing the things that bother

you to make a statement that these things can be fixed.

6. **Not Letting Go of Issues:** When working through a conflict, it can spiral very quickly. If you notice that you are both in a negative headspace and that your issues aren't being resolved, you might have to take a step back and come back to the conversation later. When one or both of you won't let go of the issue, this means that you aren't going to be able to get past it. Letting go of it together and working to find a solution shows that you are on the same page. No one likes to fight, but pride gets in the way sometimes. It can be very difficult to admit that you were wrong.

7. **Being Silent:** Using the silent treatment is not a valid way to fix your issues. By ignoring your partner, you aren't helping the situation. Instead, you are further angering them while allowing the problem to linger, and this is all due to immaturity. When you marry someone, you need to be able to have real conversations with them, no matter how tense they are. This is how you grow and learn. Having a healthy amount of conflict in your relationship is much better than experiencing phases of silence. Learn how to talk to one another and

understand that conflict means that you both still have passion.

Chapter 7:

Recognizing Irrational Behaviors that Trigger Anxiety and Insecurity

The longer that you are in a relationship with someone, the more comfortable you become. After learning about every aspect of their personality and all of their habits, both good and bad, it is safe to say that you know your partner best. For this same reason, you will often become blind to the fact that you are being triggered by normal behaviors that cause you to act irrationally. When you are feeling anxious in your marriage, you will begin to take a second look at all of these things that you think you know about your partner. In your head, it becomes very easy to start second-guessing certain behaviors and actions. When something used to appear very normal to you, it might trigger you into a battle with insecurity that causes you to act irrationally toward your partner.

These examples might seem trivial because they are often blown out of proportion. When you start to experience relationship anxiety, these things can make their way into the foreground of your brain. Once you start to question the behaviors, they will grow in severity thanks to your building insecurity. It can become a very toxic cycle if you are not careful. This is why being able to recognize when you are acting irrationally can do a lot for your marriage. By calming down and realizing what is factual and what is fueled by anxiety, both you and your partner will be a lot happier together. This kind of behavior can very easily tear a relationship apart if you let it. Being proactive; noticing if you are triggered by these things will show you a lot about what must be done to improve your relationship.

Examples

When Your Partner Doesn't Immediately Reply to Your Text

It is likely that the two of you text frequently. Texting has become a huge part of our lives in the last few decades, creating an instantaneous way to stay in touch with those we care about. When you and your partner are not together, texting can easily reconnect you and allow you to check on one another. It can be a very helpful way to communicate, but you must be aware of the pressure that it is placing on your relationship. Texting can actually lead to a lot of relationship anxiety, and this typically depends on how fast your partner replies to you.

When you are already experiencing relationship anxiety, any delay in communication with your partner is likely to send you into a spiral of irrational thoughts. You might jump to conclusions and think that they are cheating on you or that they do not want to talk to you. Stop and think about where your partner is and what they could be doing. There are likely endless possibilities. Instead of jumping to the very worst conclusion, ground yourself with a reminder that your partner could simply be busy. Whether they are out running errands, at work, or even driving, it might not be possible for them to get on their phone to text you at that moment.

Obsessing over something like this is only going to leave you feeling sick. It can even get to such an extreme that you start to fear that your partner has been hurt or has died. This is not a healthy way to live as you are waiting for a reply from the other person. Once they text you back, all of the negative feelings likely flee, only further proving the point that you were feeling these things as a part of your temporary anxiety. Try to calm yourself down as much as possible by using only rational and logical thinking. Do not be controlling or angry when they do not reply right away.

When Your Partner Can't Spend Time with You

As a couple, you likely spend a lot of quality time together. By living together, this also increases the amount of time that you get to be around one another. When you get upset with your partner for not wanting to, or not being able to, spend time together, then you are going to be placing a lot of pressure on your relationship. There are many valid reasons as to why your partner can't spend time with you. They might not have the energy because of a busy day at work, or they might have planned a night out with their friends. Understand that your partner is their own person too, not only your significant other.

When you can't spend time together, this doesn't mean that your love is fleeting. This also doesn't mean that your partner's feelings for you have changed. Being able to live your own lives while also being together is a sign of a healthy relationship. You both deserve to have friends and personal time outside of your relationship. Not always assuming that you are going to do everything together allows you to appreciate the quality time that you do have.

Know that it is perfectly normal for couples to spend time apart, even if it is only for a few hours at a time. Don't allow your mind to jump to conclusions. When your partner says that they are not able to spend time together, take that for what it is. Do not assume that you have done anything wrong or that you need to push them to be with you. Allow your love to blossom naturally. Anything that is forced in your relationship is only going to create conflicts. Remember, you do not control your significant other. They can do things on their own while still remaining loyal and faithful to you.

When Your Partner Receives a Call or Text

This is something that tends to start a lot of fights between couples, and it can become very unhealthy when it goes unaddressed — acting angry or suspicious when your partner gets a call/text is irrational behavior. When you are in a relationship, you should have a sense of trust between the two of you. Even if you can't see your partner's phone screen, you should trust that they are communicating in a way that is appropriate and respectful of your relationship. No matter who they are talking to, you should not be worrying about what your partner is saying or doing if you truly trust them. By getting worked up over this, you are only going to become obsessive each time their phone goes off.

Demanding to know who your partner is talking to at all times is taking away their right to privacy. Your anxiety can lead them to feel that they are being controlled, which is very unhealthy for any relationship. There is nothing wrong with asking your partner who they are talking to or what they are saying, but remember that they also deserve privacy. When you give your partner privacy, you are showing them that your trust in them is strong. Privacy does not equate to not caring. Instead, it shows that your relationship is stronger than your anxiety. While you might be curious, you can't allow it to get the best of you.

Remind yourself of the commitment that you made to one another. This should not have to be renewed each time that your partner responds to a text message. Your partner's feelings are not going to change in a matter of seconds. Keep all of those irrational thoughts at bay and try your best to remain calm. If you do not have a valid reason to suspect that anything is wrong, you need to take your partner's word for it. It can be maddening to tell someone that everything is okay, yet they never believe you. The feeling becomes even worse when you try to take matters into your own hands. At no point in time should you ever secretly look through your partner's phone. This is a huge violation of anyone's privacy.

When Your Partner Appears to Be Distant

In your relationship, there are times when you likely just do not feel like talking. This does not mean that your partner has done anything wrong, but it is a valid feeling that you should acknowledge. In life, anything is possible. With all of the stressors that we experience through any given day, this can be enough to lead us to a temporarily reclusive state of being. Sometimes, being quiet and alone is what we need to recharge. As you remind yourself that it is okay to feel this way, also remind yourself that your partner is going to feel this way too sometimes. Not wanting to talk or engage with your significant other does not always mean that they have done something unfavorable or that something is wrong.

By getting out of the mindset that things are always your fault, you will be able to better understand your partner. Know that you can offer your help or guidance, but they still might require some alone time to sort through their feelings. As long as you are able to offer your support, you are a great partner. You will be an even greater partner by respecting their wishes. Do not push your partner into talking to you or being around you after they have already expressed that they need distance. Take away your negative connotations with the idea of needing distance, as it is a healthy human behavior. Being with one another 24/7 isn't realistic, even if you are married and living together. You are both going to need your own space sometimes. Instead of worrying about what the problem is or what you did wrong, you can really step it up by being there for your partner when they express that they need you.

When Your Partner Takes Jokes Too Far

Couples who are able to maintain a sense of humor together often have a very fun and fulfilling relationship. Being able to joke with the person that you are closest to can be very amusing, especially when you know so much about one another. The thing about joking around is that you still need to have boundaries, even with your significant other. When you are being comical, remember that both of you should be laughing. If one person is highly amused while the other is being hurt, then this is not funny. Speak up if your partner takes any joking around too far. By letting it go on, you are only going to be encouraging this behavior. Plus, your partner truly might not have even realized that it upset you. This is why you need to speak up for yourself.

Alternatively, you also need to understand that your partner might ask the same of you. Do not take this personally, allowing your anxiety to tell you that your partner does not love you anymore because you joke around too much. Listen to what they are saying and understand that you might have hurt their feelings. This is not the end of your relationship, but it should be the end of the behavior that caused them to feel this way. Jokes that get taken too far are often based on truths that have not yet been spoken. If you have something important to say, have a proper conversation about it.

Any pending issues need to be worked through, not turned into comedy. Know that there is a time and a place for everything. When you are so close to someone, you can't take everything so personally. This is a hard thing to remember, but it will help you manage your anxiety.

When Your Partner Won't Propose to You

For many women, the thought of a significant other delaying a proposal can often lead to anxiety. Doubts will begin to come to mind, wondering if their partner truly wants to commit and questioning why a proposal has yet to happen. Even when both partners agree that they would like to get married, the thought of when this is going to happen can be nerve-wracking. For a lot of men, the pressures are different. Because men tend to be the ones to propose, they usually delay because they are waiting for the right moment. This time in between can be stressful for some couples, causing tension and conflict.

If you have relationship anxiety, all of these feelings can be heightened. You might drive yourself crazy wondering if your partner still sees you as marriage material and questioning why they haven't made the commitment yet. Instead of letting your anxiety turn into insecurity, bring up a conversation with your partner. Without pressuring your partner into proposing, you can discuss your feelings on the topic and get some reassurance that marriage is something that you both still want.

When there is any type of delay in a marriage proposal, it is usually due to the fact that the man wants to live up to the woman's expectations. He will hear about the woman's dream proposal and might feel as though he cannot make it as perfect as she wants it to be. Alternatively, the longer that the woman is waiting to be proposed to, the more she will let the doubts start to creep in. Instead of considering that her partner is trying to make it as wonderful as possible, she might be led to feelings of anxiety and doubt. This situation can easily spiral downward when it really doesn't have to. As long as you know that you are both on the same page, patience should be exercised.

Chapter 8:

How Do You Stop Being Anxious and Insecure in a Relationship?

When you are given techniques that are proven to be successful, you will be able to put your anxiety to rest. In many cases, not knowing what to do with the anxiety that you feel can lead to several different emotions. One minute, you might feel that you and your partner have a wonderful relationship, and the next you might be doubtful of everything that you share. This chapter focuses on real methods that you can use in your own life. They will help you manage your anxiety while keeping you focused on the positive reality of your relationship. Everyone experiences anxiety at some point, but it doesn't have to rule over you. Being able to set it aside and focus on making your relationship grow is ideal.

Without traveling too far outside of your comfort zone, you will learn how to combat these feelings in the easiest ways possible. Instead of fighting with your anxious thoughts or trying to push them aside, you will learn how to deal with them head-on. Through practical problem-solving, you will realize that it is never as bad as your mind wants you to believe it is. Anxiety is one of the most powerful mental forces that you can experience. It can even alter the way that you view your reality. Once you are able to see past this, you will feel empowered and ready to take on any challenge that you face. This kind of awareness makes you a better partner and allows you to have a more fulfilling relationship.

Strategies and Exercises

1. Starting with your physical body, you can actually do a lot for your anxiety by making sure

that you are getting enough exercise. When you get up and move, this allows endorphins to run through you. Endorphins make you feel good, and it is very healthy to select activities each day that boost your levels. Being mindful while paired with engaging in this physical activity will also give you a new perspective on the things that you are worried about. Staying caught up in your head can promote a clouded mindset. When you take the time to clear your mind and body, you are going to feel the difference.

Exercise can be done alone or with your partner. Having alone time is essential to any relationship, but getting active with your partner can also have its benefits. Try both! When the focus is on something entirely different, your relationship anxiety is naturally going to subside. It can be very beneficial for you to change your mindset, even if it is only for an hour while you are exercising.

When you exercise, this changes your perspective automatically. It is a way to take your mind off of your life, and instead, to focus on the exercise or activity that you are doing. Even if you aren't big on going to the gym, you can find other ways that you can get your exercise in at home or through classes. There are endless options that can actually be a lot of fun.

2. When you get into your moments of anxiety, don't suppress them! Talk to your partner about what you are feeling, even if you think that it's stupid. Your feelings should always be valid in your relationship, so your partner shouldn't make you feel stupid for sharing them. Your partner should be there for you during these moments where you are struggling. While they should not have to act as your therapist, having support from your significant other is not a lot to ask for in a relationship. If they were to have the same kind of anxiety and worries, you would be there for them as well.

Even if your partner cannot help you fix your problems, they can provide you with an outlet and help you tackle them. When you speak out loud about your issues, this takes away their power. By having someone who simply understands you, or tries to see where you are coming from, this can allow you to feel less alone as you try to find solutions to fix your problems. This is what a healthy relationship should look like. Keep in mind that your partner might not be able to help you actually heal from your anxiety, but their support should not go unnoticed. When you can be candid about your insecurities, this is going to help your relationship grow. It will show your partner that you are willing to work on your downfalls.

3. Letting go of control can be extremely difficult, especially when you are struggling. Know that it is essential that you are able to let go of this control though. Your anxiety is going to be telling you that you need to have more control or something bad is going to happen. When you accept that you actually cannot control everything, you will be able to work on ways that you can make the good moments even better and deal with the bad ones. Instead of thinking about your life as a doomsday situation, bring yourself back down to reality. Realize that this isn't a matter of life or death and that you are going to be okay.

When you are so consumed by the thought of having control over your life, this definitely impacts your relationship. Your partner might need you, yet you will only be able to see the things that pertain to your control issues. Whether you are bummed about having to work late or a friend getting upset with you, know that these are not situations that should completely derail you. Know that you will get through them, and you can vent to your partner if you need to. There is a difference between talking about the things that get you down and letting them completely take over your life and your decisions. When you learn how to let go of your control, you are actually going to feel a lot more free in your life.

4. When you are in your anxiety mode, your reactions to certain things are going to be a lot different than your normal reactions. Learn how to recognize when you are acting out of anxiety. This is going to help you correct your behavior and allow yourself to get grounded once again. Listen to your partner if they ever tell you that they think you are acting irrationally. As you know, anxiety can often lead to irrational behavior. You should not take this personally, as this hint can actually tell you that you might be letting your anxiety take over your life. Also, know that your partner is telling you this because they care about you and want you to be healthy.

Everything that you do is going to end up impacting your partner in some way. While they might not be able to feel the relationship anxiety that you feel, they are going to notice a difference in your behavior when you are experiencing it. You might be easily angered or even more clingy, but these behaviors should be fairly easy to spot. When you get the hang of identifying them, you can then set your focus on how to put your anxiety to rest. Try to compare and contrast; once your anxiety passes, ask yourself if you would have acted the same way or if you would act differently now. You might find that your reactions are entirely different when anxiety isn't pressuring you.

5. Anxiety comes along with triggers. These are things that can send you into anxious moods or behaviors. A trigger can be something that reminds you of an event that you once went through or just something that causes you to feel insecure. Everyone has different triggers, and there is nothing wrong with this. You cannot help it because they are triggering to you based on what you have experienced in your life. While you cannot avoid them in your daily life, you can make your partner aware of them to help strengthen your relationship. When you inform them of the things that upset you and why, you are allowing them in and shedding light on the issues.

If you find that you are constantly being triggered by things that your partner does, yet you do not let them know, this becomes unfair. You are going to feel upset all the time, and your partner isn't going to know what they are doing wrong. To help this situation, you need to rely on your communication skills. See how important they are and make sure that you do not take them for granted. When you tell your partner about your triggers, try your best to explain each one. To do so, you need to get to the roots of your issues. With enough practice, this shouldn't be too difficult. Place a priority on honesty and openness; it will make a difference.

6. In terms of reassurance, physical affection can do a lot to ease your anxiety. Even something as simple as holding hands can remind you of how great your relationship is and how much your partner loves you. While you should not solely rely on physical intimacy to know that your partner cares, it can be a welcome reminder during the times when you are plagued with anxiety. Without being overly clingy, you and your partner can regain your closeness by displaying a little bit of affection for one another. Know that they likely want reassurance just as much as you do. Even if you are already well past your honeymoon stage, physical affection can remind you about the things that you love about one another.

It isn't wrong to ask your partner for physical affection. Just because they are not being physically affectionate does not mean that they do not want to be. By asking for a hug or asking to cuddle, your partner might realize that they really wanted and needed the intimacy, yet they were distracted by other things in life. This can happen very easily. The longer you are together, the easier it becomes to take physical affection for granted. When you can rekindle the feeling, you are going to feel very loved and very close to one another. Do your best to show one another small acts of affection on a daily basis to keep the intimacy strong.

7. Having a standard in your mind of what your relationship *should* look like or *should* be like is going to become very damaging to how your relationship actually operates. Try your best not to compare your partner or your relationship to the things that you see around you. Each relationship is unique and made up of entirely different people. Instead of placing a comparison on your relationship, do your best to see the great qualities that you share with your partner. Learn how to appreciate them for who they are and respect the things that they love. When you two are able to be completely genuine and comfortable with one another, this is going to create a great foundation for your relationship.

There is no such thing as perfect. If you are only trying to strive for perfection, this is likely going to drive you straight to a state of anxiety. Know that you do not have to maintain your relationship in a certain way to impress other people. Many people admit to making their relationship appear better than it actually is because they do not want others to know that they face problems. Every single couple faces problems. It is not realistic to always get along and live in harmony with your spouse; you are two different people! What matters is how you work through these issues, as you cannot let them divide you. Know that you don't have to impress or convince anyone of your happiness; just be happy.

8. A very valuable option for getting help with your relationship anxiety is to seek therapy. When you see a therapist, you have the option to get all of your anxious thoughts out of your head. This is what the therapist is there for. When you are able to sort through your issues, this is not only going to make you a better person but a better partner. Know that you can see a therapist on your own, or you can begin couples therapy with your partner. Both are going to have their own benefits. In individual therapy, you will be speaking on your problems from your perspective. The focus will mainly be on you. Engaging in couple's therapy will allow both yourself and your partner to have your own voices.

A lot of stigma is placed around getting help for your mental health, but know that this judgment should not hinder you from getting help. If you think that therapy might be the answer, or if you are curious to try it, listen to your gut instinct. The opinions of others should not be able to dictate what you can and cannot do in your life. By taking back control over what you are doing, this is going to allow you to feel that you truly can tackle your anxiety. A lot of people find that it is just too hard to deal with their anxiety without this outside help. If you are one of them, know that this isn't shameful!

Chapter 9:

How to Use Your Relationship Anxiety to Grow

All of the exercises that were provided in the previous chapter follow a certain theme — putting the anxiety in its place. When you can decide how you are going to live your life and how you are going to interact with your partner, you will be a lot happier with the decisions that you make. Your anxiety does not have to control you, so don't give in! In this chapter, you are going to focus on how to use your relationship anxiety to grow. When you can turn your hardships into a way to become a better person and a better partner, this is a true sign of growth. It can seem difficult to get your anxiety under control, but you should also know by now that it is not impossible. When you can find the strategies that work for you, this will show you a small beacon of hope and how your anxiety does not always have to lead you.

Establish a Deeper Connection

When you first began dating your partner, there was likely a lot to talk about. That early stage of any relationship is typically bustling with conversation and the desire to put in the effort to impress one another. This honeymoon stage is something that all couples know is fleeting, but it doesn't have to disappear entirely. Even when you already know everything about your partner, try not to lose interest in them. People can change and grow, so you actually probably don't know everything about your partner. Show them that you still care to know new things and that you still find them just as interesting as you did when you first began dating.

Your connection with one another is limitless. This is the person that you have chosen to spend the rest of your life with, so make sure that you are still able to show them how much you care and how much they intrigue you. When couples lose this magic, the relationship can very quickly become stale. This will often trigger a great deal of relationship anxiety. Not all relationships must fizzle out just because you have been together for a long time. You still need to put in the effort for one another if you want to be in a thriving relationship. It takes work that you must be willing to constantly improve on. Keep learning about what your partner needs from you and think about new ways to give that to them.

When you have an ever-growing connection with your partner, this is going to promote healthy communication skills and excellent conflict resolution skills. In turn, this also strengthens your trust. Overall, you can see that deepening your connection with your partner is going to provide many benefits for the relationship. By having a clear awareness of what one another needs from the relationship, you will both be able to become the best partners that you can be. Understand the ways in which relationships evolve over time. Nothing is going to stay the same forever, but this does not mean that your love or connection will be lost. By accepting these changes, you will be able to learn the ways that you need to grow and work on yourself to adapt.

This is a very powerful way in which you can take your relationship anxiety and turn it around to better serve you. If you feel that you are becoming disconnected from your partner, it is not too late to rebuild your relationship. Having an honest conversation can do a lot for the two of you. Even if you don't want to get into a heavy issue, you can be candid about something that is more lighthearted. By getting back into the habit of regularly communicating with your partner, they are likely going to follow suit. When you can both bounce these ideas off of one another, back and forth, you are creating something that will allow you to bond. Listen to your needs and don't be afraid to ask your partner for more if you require it.

Spend Quality Time Together

Learn about what is important to your partner, from their hobbies to their passions. When you two can spend quality time doing these things together, it will bring you closer together. You will also have a better understanding of who your partner is. It feels great when someone cares to learn about the things that you enjoy doing, so give this feeling to your partner whenever possible. Instead of worrying about what your partner might be thinking or desiring, you can learn about what they actually want. This will allow you some relief with your relationship anxiety. The anxiety stems from a fear of the unknown, so it makes sense that you would feel better when you know exactly what your partner loves to do.

There is a fine line between bonding with your partner and forcing yourself to do things that you do not enjoy.

You are doing to have differences in what each of you finds enjoyable, but when you can find some commonalities, then you are going to be able to become even closer. Just because you are a couple does not mean that you are required to do everything together. Try new things because you want to, not because you feel that you have to force yourself to do them. This will show your partner that you are genuinely interested in doing things that they enjoy without compromising your own interests and passions. If you are having trouble finding common ground, you can even seek out brand new activities that you have both never tried before. Discovering life this way will allow you to grow even closer to your partner. It will allow your anxiety to subside while you are both having fun in the process.

It is a very motivational feeling when you can still find new and exciting things to do with your significant other, even when you have already been dating for a while. Life doesn't have to become boring just because you are married or in a long-term relationship. Having a sense of adventure is going to keep the magic alive. The worst thing that can happen is you will discover that you do not enjoy doing these activities. When this happens, you can come together to try to discover other things that you both want to do. Couples often forget that the discovery process does not end as the years progress. You do not have to settle into a permanent routine. While having a routine provides you with a sense of security, being open to new adventures will keep you feeling refreshed.

You'll notice that the more you try with your partner, the less you will be faced with worries that you are not good enough or exciting enough for them. Instead of succumbing to the fears that pop into your head, you will be taking action. This is going to make you feel great and show your partner that you are invested in the relationship. Couples who have fun together are less likely to get into arguments over trivial things. You will both be able to realize that there is a lot more out there that you can do together to keep your bond strong and to keep your relationship feeling how it did in the beginning.

Go the Extra Mile

Your anxiety can either drive you to a breaking point or motivate you into making a change. When you are willing to go the extra mile for your partner, you can tune out of the same fears that keep popping up in your mind. For example, you can continuously think of new ways to show your partner love and affection without being clingy, as your anxiety might suggest you need to be. Instead of smothering them, do things that are thoughtful and considerate based on their needs. Cooking a meal for your spouse or cleaning up their bedside table can be a simple yet effective way to show them how much you care.

It is important to be true to yourself while you are doing kind things for your partner. If you get to the point where you are sacrificing your own happiness to make your significant other happy, then this is just as unhealthy as letting the anxiety take over. You need to find the right balance that makes sense in your relationship. When you want to do something nice for your partner, think about the little things that you can achieve quickly. Sometimes, less is more when you want to add extra effort into your relationship.

Make sure that you still go on dates. Having a regular date night can be very beneficial to your relationship. Try new restaurants that you've always wanted to try, spend a night exploring your own city, or see two movies back-to-back. There are countless ways that you can have a date with your partner without falling into the same old routines that you are used to. When you do something different, you are showing your partner that you are putting in some extra effort. Instead of focusing on the extravagant things that you want to do together, know that these little things will add up. You can take your relationship further than ever before by incorporating these small gestures into your regular routines.

If something reminds you of your partner, let them know. It can be really nice to hear that your spouse is thinking about you when you aren't together. This showcases your closeness and your bond. It is also a nice way to check-in with one another to see how your days are going. Your goal should be to keep the romance alive. Instead of worrying that the romance is already gone, as your anxiety wants to lead you to believe, you can prove that your relationship is much stronger than your worries. Tell yourself that what you have with your partner is special and then do your best to cultivate it every single day.

When you can prove to yourself that you are enough, your worries will begin to listen to you. Negative thinking can put you into a very dark mindset very quickly. Before you know it, you will have a very warped perception of your own relationship. Focusing on the good things that you know you share with your partner is going to serve as a reminder of why you should always aim to keep improving your relationship. No one else is going to be able to convince you of this except for yourself.

Learn about the Warning System

If you just can't seem to shake your anxiety, there is something that you can do to put a positive spin on it. By becoming great at recognizing your triggers and irrational behaviors, you will also be able to see your anxiety as a built-in warning system. This means that you should be able to recognize your anxious thoughts as an alarm telling you that you need to reframe your thinking. Whether you are being triggered by something or just obsessing over something, this is an indication that you are too deep in your head. Consider if you are seeing your own relationship and your own partner clearly. Confirm that you understand exactly where your thoughts and feelings are coming from. By taking a moment to reflect on this, it can save you a lot of hardship when your anxiety does flare up.

Breathing is so important. Whenever you get really worked up over something that your anxiety creates, take some time to just breathe before you react. When you can stop to breathe, you can also empty your mind. Think about the things that are factual and true. Anything based on worry, fear, or insecurity can be set aside for the moment. This is going to guide you toward the strategy you should already be familiar with — getting to the root of the issue. With a clear mind, you will be able to make more rational decisions.

Your anxiety triggers your fight-or-flight response. No matter which action you take, it is usually one that is based on fear-driven rationality. Instead of living your life based on where your fears take you, try to shift this focus. You can remember the things that make you happy, the things that you are passionate about. Once you have your sights set back onto these things of importance, you will be able to make a much better decision on what to do next. It takes a lot of self-discipline to not give in to the anxiety as soon as you feel it, but it is going to help you tremendously once you are able to see that you *can* control yourself.

Don't be so hard on yourself when you do realize that you are feeling anxious. Remember, you can't help that you have relationship anxiety. The only thing that you can do is work with your symptoms and focus on the good things that you already have going for you. This will automatically put you in a more positive mindset that will make you a better partner in return. Those who live their lives while making thoughtful decisions are often happier with the outcomes of said decisions. You will feel that your choices are made deliberately instead of feeling that these things are simply happening to you.

Chapter 10:

Improving Self-Awareness and Self-Passion with Anxiety in a Relationship

While the focus so far has been on how to be a better partner while dealing with relationship anxiety, know that your own feelings are also very important. If you do not like the person you are becoming because of the anxiety that you are facing, know that you are not alone. A lot of people struggle with their own self-worth when they experience relationship anxiety because it can become very easy to punish yourself over your actions. Instead of focusing on the things that you are bad at or the things that you are doing wrong, this chapter is going to teach you how to be kinder to yourself. When you are constantly putting yourself down, this is only going to become more stressful and promote more anxiety. The way that you use your inner-voice can make a big difference in the way that you make your future decisions.

Before you begin with these exercises, make sure that you are in the right mindset to work on yourself. Understand that you deserve kindness and respect, just as your partner does. Make a promise that you are no longer going to tear yourself down or disrespect yourself just because you are struggling. Instead, you must focus on compassion. If your partner were going through a hard time, it is much more likely that you would act compassionately rather than angrily. Try to uphold these same standards for the way that you treat yourself. It sends a very conflicting message to your brain when you are being so kind to your partner yet so horrible to yourself.

Being kind to yourself can be a lot harder than it seems. It might take you a long time to get out of your negative headspace, but that is okay. Another skill that you are going to have to use is patience. Be patient with yourself and understand that this is going to be a process. You cannot expect results after only one day of positive thinking. However, when you put in the effort each day, you are going to end up seeing results. You are only going to get here by believing in yourself and believing in the process. If you are tired of being ruled by your anxiety, this is all the reason that you need to make a change for the better. Use this as a motivational tool to help you improve yourself. Remind yourself of how hard it can be to constantly feel that you have to answer to your anxiety before you do things.

It can be hard to commit to focusing on yourself, especially when you haven't been very kind to yourself lately. This chapter is going to teach you how to get back to these basics of self-care. It is not uncommon that people forget how to care for themselves when they enter a serious relationship. The focus tends to shift on the other person so much that it can be very easy to lose your own sense of what you need to be happy. Putting a stop to this imbalance as soon as you notice it will also help keep your relationship intact. When your partner sees how much you are doing for them, yet can also see that you are neglecting yourself, this can put pressure on them and on your relationship. For anything to be harmonious, it must be balanced first.

Accept that Anxiety is Common

The first step to working on yourself comes when you are able to let go of any guilt that you might be holding onto. You are not the only person who has felt relationship anxiety before; that is a fact. No matter how great your relationship or your partner is, you can still experience relationship anxiety. This is not your fault, and it is definitely not something that you need to punish yourself for. Before you get angry or frustrated with yourself for feeling the way that you do, stop to think about what this negativity is going to do for your relationship anxiety. Is it going to make it better? The more likely answer is that it is going to stress you out even more, causing you even more anxiety.

People experience relationship anxiety because they just want to be loved. This is one of the most universal human desires that you can experience. It is normal and healthy to desire love because love allows you to feel whole. While you don't need it to survive, having it in your life is very fulfilling. Before you can expect others to love you, it is important that you can love yourself. Try to recognize the amazing qualities that you have to offer. Write down all of the strengths that you have and read the list when you start to sink into a negative mindset. It might be uncomfortable to give yourself this much praise, but this is how you are going to grow. By acknowledging all of these great things about yourself, it will become easier for you to see what your partner sees in you.

If it helps you, speak to your friends and loved ones who also suffer from relationship anxiety. Knowing that you're not alone can provide you with a calming sense of solidarity. Being open to these conversations will normalize the idea of relationship anxiety, further proving that it is nothing for you to feel shame or guilt over. When you can talk to someone other than your significant other who experiences the same things that you do, it might be easier to think about ways that you can handle it. Seek advice and inspiration from those around you.

Wanting to be happy is not something that you should feel wrong for wanting. As long as you are being good to your partner and being good to yourself, there should be no reason why you must hold yourself back from experiencing happiness. The negative voices in your head might be telling you otherwise, but know that you have so much power within. You have the power to silence these voices and to prove that you are worthy of love and happiness. The power behind positive thinking is amazing once you get the hang of it.

Practice Mindfulness

Being mindful is not the same thing as being self-centered. Many people are under the misconception that mindfulness makes you a selfish person. In fact, it makes you the opposite! When you are mindful, this means that you have a heightened sense of awareness and understanding of what is going on around you. This all begins from within, being mindful of the way you are feeling and why. When you can show yourself some empathy, you will be able to do the same for your partner. As mentioned, it sends your brain a confusing message when you are kind to your partner yet degrading to yourself. Your actions need to match your words.

It can be hard to get into the mindset of mindful thinking, especially when the daily tasks of life are pressuring you into thinking about other things. No matter what you have going on each day, devote at least 10 minutes of time in which you can be by yourself. With this time, you are going to work on your mindfulness. The easiest way to do this is by meditating. You do not have to take a yoga class to receive all of the benefits of meditation. Sitting alone in a dimly lit room for these 10 minutes can be enough to shift your way of thinking. Try your best to empty your head as you meditate, imagining that you are being surrounded by a warm ball of light. At the end of your meditation, leave yourself with a positive affirmation about yourself.

Forgiveness is another way to practice mindfulness. You must be able to forgive yourself, just as you are able to forgive others. When you make a mistake, acknowledge that you could have done better without putting yourself down. Think about the things that you can do next time to improve yourself. If you are constantly punishing yourself when you make mistakes, there will be no lessons learned. Mistakes give you an opportunity to do better and to be better. Realize that you need to be constructive with your criticism. Don't let your anxiety get the best of you by pushing you into a negative string of emotions.

When you begin to live as a mindful individual, the little things that once bothered you so much won't hold the same weight. While you might face inconveniences and hard times, you need to always look at the bigger picture. Remember to be thankful for the things that you already have. Counting your blessings each day is another way to remain mindful. It can be so easy to focus on what is wrong that you will start to forget what is right and what is stable. These pillars of stability will provide you with the strength that you need to move forward. Lean on them when you are in need.

Seek Outlets for Your Thoughts

While you can talk to your partner about the way that you are feeling, know that you should not make them your therapist. This is an unfair position to put anyone in, especially the person that you are romantically involved with. Other people, including your partner, are only going to be able to listen to your problems and provide you with advice if they feel that they can relate to these things. They want the best for you, but you have to want the best for you too. Realize that there are other outlets that you can utilize when your anxious thoughts become overwhelming. Going to therapy is a very valuable experience that you should give yourself the opportunity to try. As mentioned, therapy is a very good way to work on yourself with the help of an individual who only has your best interest in mind.

There are other ways that you can express yourself. Writing can be a very healing method to try. When you journal each day, you are allowing a place to store your thoughts. Think about your journaling as a release. Once the negativity and anxiety are placed onto the page, let it stay there. The more that you practice letting go of things, the less likely they are going to be able to torment you later. Clearing your mind will make room for new thoughts and better mindsets. Those who feel that they cannot open up to self-love usually don't have any room to think positively.

Exercise can be another great outlet for you to use. You know how great endorphins can make you feel and when you exercise, you are giving yourself something else to focus on. By turning your attention toward your physical health, your mental health is also going to improve. Sometimes, it takes a little bit of physical activity to remind you that there are other ways that you can take care of yourself. Without the health of your physical body, you would not be able to do much. This is why eating and sleeping properly also become big components of taking care of yourself.

No matter which outlet you choose, make sure that your negative thoughts are staying away once you release them. If you need to, use an outlet more than once to truly get the anxiety out of your head. It might be necessary, but that doesn't make it any less effective. Anxiety can be very stubborn and clingy, but you do not need to give in. Know that you are strong enough to face any thought that comes to your mind, so don't fret if you need to try several times before you feel that you are truly making a difference. The self-love journey is going to become a lifelong journey for you.

Fall in Love with Yourself

Self-love will take practice. If you are having trouble being kind to yourself, you are not alone. Many people find this difficult because it makes them uncomfortable. You must understand that self-love is not selfish. It is within your right to be proud of yourself and to be kind to yourself. If you cannot get to this point right away, you need to remember to be gentle with yourself. Anxiety responds to stress and any added stress in your life is going to make your anxiety a lot worse. If you can eliminate some of the anxiety that you experience by simply being nicer to yourself, then you will see how self-love can be a great tool to use when you are going through a difficult time.

To do this, you must step outside of your comfort zone. If you have a hard time accepting compliments or saying kind things about yourself, this exercise is going to get you in a different mindset. Sit down with a piece of paper and a pen. Put on a 10-minute timer and don't stop writing kind things about yourself until that timer goes off. Do not think too hard about what you write down. These ideas should come to you naturally. When you list the first things that come to mind, you will be able to see an idea of what you really think about yourself. There is always going to be room for improvement, but it is important that you can identify the things that you are proud of yourself for at the moment.

Spend some time with yourself outside of the house. The great thing about alone time is that you can do exactly what you want when you want. Do something that you have been wanting to do for a long time, something that you truly enjoy. When you can be your true self, you are going to be able to see more reasons why you should love yourself. Even around your spouse, there might be times when you feel that you have to hold back from what you are saying or thinking. This happens when you care about people and don't want to upset them. By spending time with yourself, you are really going to get to know yourself.

Some people become really uncomfortable with the thought of being alone because their anxiety mistakenly informs them that they cannot survive without their partner or their relationship. While your partner can feel like your other half, make sure that you know you are still a whole person without them. You have your own hobbies and interests. Your personality is unique to you. Those who get into the codependent mindset usually have a harder time breaking free of their anxiety and loving themselves.

Understand External Influences

Did you know that there are other factors that can contribute to your relationship anxiety? People and situations that exist outside of your marriage can actually give you anxiety. Whether it is a friend with a strong opinion of how you are living your life or pressure that you are feeling from your family, these outside forces actually have a lot to do with the anxiety that you experience within your relationship. Without being too guarded, you always need to protect yourself from these outside factors. There are plenty of other people in your life whom you love and respect, but know that they have the ability to hurt you as well. While working on protecting yourself, you should also work on standing up for yourself.

When you find that something or someone external is impacting your relationship, put a barrier up between the stressor and the relationship. The only people who truly have a say in the relationship are you and your partner. Other people can become very opinionated, but this does not mean that they should dictate anything about your life or your love life. Work on setting these boundaries, not only because you respect your relationship but because you respect your partner. When a couple does not have boundaries like this in place, they often struggle with conflicts that arise due to issues that other people start.

Getting a handle on the issues that you and your partner face might lead you to realize that it is the external factors causing your stress. By letting go of the outside noise that you cannot control, you will likely find a lot of relief for your anxiety. Unfortunately, you aren't always going to be able to eliminate these stressors, but you do have the ability to control how you react. When you are secure in yourself and your relationship, it leaves little room for anxiety to develop, especially anxiety that is caused by outside forces. Before you react unfavorably to something, consider if it is worth your time and energy. Is there anything else that you could be doing that would be more fulfilling or productive?

You and your partner can actually bond when you both realize that these outside forces cannot hinder your relationship. Couples who get worked up over these things often end up in fights that stem from things that they cannot change. When you two can work together as a team, you are going to feel a lot more secure in your relationship. Remember, you should both be on the same page and working toward the same goals. When you feel that you and your partner are divided, you can work on ways to regain closeness and remind yourself that you both want the same things. Focus on your love and your happiness.

Work on Self-Care

You've heard the term mentioned several times so far, but you might still be wondering one thing — what qualifies as self-care? Anything that you do that allows you to have fun or relax with the sole purpose of making yourself feel good is self-care. This is going to vary for people because everyone has different interests. You might enjoy spending time alone at home, while others might enjoy going out and doing things outside of the house. No matter where you go or what you do, the self-care methods that you select should help you feel happy and stable.

Aside from the activities that you do with yourself, also focus on eating and sleeping better. What you eat and how much you sleep both impact your self-care routine greatly. If you are exhausted and not nourishing yourself properly, this is going to naturally lead you to a bad mood. Your brain and body cannot function without a healthy eating and sleeping routine. Make it a point to go to bed 30 minutes earlier and to eat more fresh fruits and vegetables each day. Small changes that are made consistently will help make a difference in your overall goal of self-care.

If you still feel that your anxiety is flaring up while you are practicing self-care, consider that you might be loading your body with vices that are making you feel anxious. Do you drink coffee? Alcohol? Do you smoke? Any of these things can be habit-forming, causing your mind and body to feel that they are dependent on them. Try your best to work through your vices, showing your body that you can survive without any of them. This is going to be a process, but you will feel a lot better when you can be free of any demanding habits.

You might begin to feel guilty when you practice self-care because you aren't thinking about your relationship as much as you used to. This is okay! It is normal to take a break from thinking about your love life and your partner to better focus on yourself. This does not make you a bad or neglectful partner. Realize that your own needs are important, too. You are your own person, and it is okay that you need time for yourself.

Through the different activities that you decide to do with yourself, you will realize that you probably have a lot of work to do. Many are surprised to find that they are in healthy relationships, yet the one they need to improve is their relationship with themselves. As you work through this journey of self-care, it can be a good idea to write down how you are feeling. This will allow you to have something to compare your current feelings to when you begin to make progress.

Rewire Your Brain

When you feel yourself jumping to the worst possible conclusion, step in and tell your brain that this is irrational. Unless you have been given clear signs that something is devastatingly wrong, then there is no reason for you to stress yourself out. Begin breathing exercises as soon as you can feel your brain jumping to conclusions. Take several deep breaths to get centered. Now, think about what you were originally worried about. Understand that you are likely reacting this way because the situation is out of your control; you must accept this. To soothe your nerves, think about the things that you *can* control. This should be easy because you will realize that you can control your own actions. So, what are you going to do that will allow you to feel better and to remain calm?

If you need to use reason, you can think about realistic outcomes of the situation that you are worried about. Understand that there is only so much that you can do, so there is no point in getting yourself worked up to the point where you experience anxiety. Distractions can also be welcome when you are trying to avoid anxiety. Self-care can be a very nice way to distract yourself because it is also productive. When you can work on yourself and loving yourself, you will be able to feel better about the little things that once worried you.

Your goal is to rewire your brain. When an anxious thought threatens to take over, you need to replace it with something that is more positive. Whether it is a thought about self-love or something that you are looking forward to, you need to give yourself encouragement that it is okay to stop thinking about your relationship to spare your mental health. The more that you learn how to replace your negative thoughts, the better you will begin to feel. You do not have to give in to anxiety, even when it is very persistent.

If you begin to feel insecure in your relationship because of your anxiety, remember the great exercises that you learned that will allow you to strengthen your relationship. Give your partner compliments and do kind things for them without any prompting. When you do things because you genuinely want to, your partner is going to feel your love. Know that your love is enough and who you are is enough. In a healthy relationship, you should feel that you don't have to change yourself to make your partner happy. You also need to be in tune with your own needs to ensure that they are also being met. It is okay to feel insecure at times; this is natural. What matters most is how you handle your insecurities. When you can see that you are a whole person with valuable qualities, you will be able to find ways to love yourself as much as you love your partner.

Conclusion

As you continue on with your relationship anxiety journey, know that you are going to have your own ups and downs. Sometimes, you might feel that you are in total control of your feelings. Other times, the anxiety is going to threaten to take over control. When you can find a balance, no matter what is going on, you are going to be a lot happier in your relationship. You should find solace in knowing that relationship anxiety is normal, and it is not your fault. Anxiety is a very powerful force that can be incredibly hard to control. Now that you understand what you can do about it, your healing journey can officially begin.

You can use this book at any time that you feel you need additional support. When the anxiety is particularly bad, you can review the different methods to combat it. There are also plenty of helpful hints throughout this book that will remind you how to refocus your energy. When you become too focused and obsessive over one thought or idea, this is going to give your anxiety an invitation to come forward. You will be able to tell right away when you are not balanced. This is going to be your number one indicator that you must make a change to preserve your mental health and the health of your relationship.

Having doubts in any relationship is normal, no matter how long you have been together or how well you know each other. What is important is how you handle your doubts. If you keep them inside and allow them to torment you, this is going to impact the way that you feel about relationship anxiety. By having an honest conversation with your partner, you will have an outlet for your doubts while simultaneously receiving reassurance. Understand that it is not up to your partner to make you feel better though. You need to be able to calm yourself down and keep yourself in check.

Your past can trigger you and this is not your fault. If you have had horrible past relationship experiences, then it makes sense that you would carry these worries into your current relationship. What you need to remember is that not every relationship is going to mirror your past experiences. Even if you have been through plenty of hardship, know that not everyone is going to treat you this way. It can be incredibly difficult to separate the past from the present, but it is going to help you a lot. Therapy can become very beneficial for this purpose.

Even if you are not being triggered by your past, you can become triggered by certain things that your partner does. They might not be doing these things intentionally, but their actions could be causing you to experience anxiety. The most important thing for you to do is to tell them as soon as you realize what is happening. When you are able to work through these things together as a couple, you will both feel that you are on the same page. Understand that it might be you who needs to change, but as long as your partner is aware of what is bothering you about their behavior, they might be able to act in a more mindful manner.

You need to create a goal to not allow your anxiety to push you into a pattern of irrational behavior. This can happen very quickly, sometimes without you even realizing that it is happening. Irrational behavior is what leads to conflict. When you start fighting with your partner, this is going to lead to even more insecurity within the relationship. When you can recognize your own irrational behavior, you will be able to prevent or correct it. Understand that this is your anxious self reacting and that you do not need to be this person all the time. Try your best to keep yourself grounded and in touch with reality. You can only focus on the things that you know are factual.

While this process sounds difficult, it can be a great way for you to reignite the spark that you have with your partner. When you can both get back in touch with the things that you love about one another, you will see that the chemistry still remains. You do not need to let your anxiety get the best of you and get in the way of your relationship. All relationships are work, and you must be willing to put in the effort. When you become stagnant, your partner is going to feel this. Try your best to help the relationship bloom, and during your weaker moments, you should be able to lean on your partner as they put their effort in. All strong relationships have an equal hand from both partners.

Thank you very much for selecting this workbook to help your relationship! Please remember to leave a great review and share all of the ways that you were able to turn your marriage around. Relationship anxiety is very strong, but remember that you are stronger! As I expressed, I have also been through this same situation. It is incredibly difficult to manage at times, but there is a light at the end of the tunnel. You do not have to remain a victim of your own relationship anxiety.

By breaking free of destructive thought patterns, you will be able to rediscover yourself and who you truly are. By allowing yourself to experience self-love, you will become a better partner by default. When times get tough, don't give up! Think about all of the progress that you have made so far. From the instant that you started reading this book, you became more educated on the topic of relationship anxiety; knowledge is power.

Do not go yet; One last thing to do...

If you enjoyed this book or found it useful I'd be very grateful if you'd post a short review on Amazon.com. Your support really does make a difference and I read all the reviews personally so I can get your feedback and make this book even better.

Thanks again for your support!

References

Birch, J. (2019, January 28). "I Have Relationship Anxiety—Here's How It Affects My Dating Life." Retrieved February 18, 2020, from https://www.health.com/relationships/relationship-anxiety

Free stock photos - Pexels. (2020). Retrieved February 19, 2020, from https://www.pexels.com/

PsychAlive. (2017, September 25). How to Deal with Relationship Anxiety. Retrieved February 18, 2020, from https://www.psychalive.org/how-to-deal-with-relationship-anxiety/

Star, K. (2019, September 29). Are There Potential Benefits to Having Anxiety? Retrieved February 18, 2020, from https://www.verywellmind.com/benefits-of-anxiety-2584134

www.ingramcontent.com/pod-product-compliance
Lightning Source LLC
Chambersburg PA
CBHW070922080526
44589CB00013B/1400